A Cathedral Renewed

A Cathedral Renewed

St Macartan's Monaghan

EDITED BY ELTIN GRIFFIN O.CARM

the columba press

First published in 1998 by
the columba press
55A Spruce Avenue, Stillorgan Industrial Park, Blackrock, Co Dublin

Designed by Bill Bolger
Photographs by John-David Biggs, except pp.71 and 74 by Peadar McMahon,
p.95 by Mildred Dunne, and p.34 which is reproduced from
A History of St Macartan's Cathedral and its Patron Saint, 1949.
Printed in Ireland by Colour Books Ltd, Dublin

ISBN 1856072517

Editor's Note

As editor of this work, I wish to record my sincere thanks to the contributors. The task was made easy by their willing acceptance and by their prompt delivery of the material. I am particularly grateful to Mary King, widow of the late Richard Enda King, and to Frances Biggs, for a lot of background information. Also to Gerald MacCann, the local architect who had supervised the entire transition from the old to the new, for his unfailing courtesy and patience. Finally to Bishop Joseph Duffy who gave me such free access to the archives and records.

Eltin Griffin O. Carm.

Contents

Introduction

Bishop charles MacNally had mixed feelings about the choice of Monaghan rather than Clogher as the eventual site of his cathedral church. In the end it was a case of a cherished tradition giving way to the harsh realities of post-Famine Ireland. Clogher was remote from the majority of his flock; there was the further difficulty of getting an appropriate site. Monaghan, on the other hand, was a county town where Catholics were gradually re-emerging and establishing themselves after the exclusion of the penal laws. It had grown originally around the ruins of a fifteenth-century Franciscan friary whose patrons were the Lucht Tighe Mhic Mhathghamhna, the MacMahon chiefs who claimed the title of Lord of Oriel or Airghialla, a medieval name for the diocese of Clogher.

Having arrived in Monaghan in 1851, Bishop MacNally set about the enormous task of planning a cathedral which would also be a parish church for the people of Monaghan, his new *lucht tighe*. Freestanding in a hilltop park of more than eight acres on the south-eastern edge of the town, his cathedral today enjoys undisputed eminence among the buildings of the town and the surrounding countryside. From any of the higher hills around, its most obvious feature is the sturdy tower and soaring spire, the latter having no purpose other than to be an elaborate decoration in the medieval Gothic style of the cathedral. It has the effect, however, of publicly identifying the building as a church, as an open house of prayer where all are welcome. More significantly, perhaps, it sends out a signal of hope to those who have become cynical these days about the claims of religion. The spire may not speak today with the unquestioned authority and certainty of the time it was built. But it keeps before us the perennial questions: Is it possible to speak meaningfully about another world? Does human history have a plan or a purpose? What can we reasonably expect from life?

If you are at home with this kind of question, you will be keen to visit the cathedral. You will also read this book with interest. You will be deeply grateful, as I am, to our accomplished editor, Father Eltin Griffin, for his outstanding success in bringing together a team to describe in some detail the manner and context in which the building was planned and recently renewed. On Confirmation Sunday this year, we unveiled a small plaque to the victims of the Great Famine in the grounds of the cathedral. The carving on the plaque was by Thomas Glendon, whose teacher, the late Michael Biggs, did so much for the reordering of the cathedral. The plaque was erected beside a long-since disused cemetery where Famine victims were reputedly buried. It records that a quarter of the entire population of the diocese of Clogher perished or emigrated during the decade of the Famine. This simple fact alone gives us a measure of the astonishing achievement of the builders of the cathedral who began the project a mere ten years later. The task took over thirty years to complete, from the laying of the foundation stone in 1861 until the dedication in 1892.

The renewal, which began in the mid-1960s, was a very different kind of experience, not without its own tensions, frustrations and occasional moments of high drama. It meant the adaptation of the interior of the cathedral to the liturgical reforms of the Vatican Council. In order to involve people actively, and to enrich their understanding of the liturgy, the reforms included a radical revision of Mass and the Sacraments. In this process the layout of the church had an important part to play. Superficially, it was about the priest facing the people and making them feel at home and part of the action. But that was only the beginning and to stop there would be to seriously misunderstand the renewed liturgy. The real challenge is not only to bring people together but to lead them together into the mysteries of faith, to reach out with them in our common human condition towards the infinite otherness of God.

The changes in the cathedral were the result of a process of extensive consultation and experimentation which began in 1965 and concluded in 1983. The initial intention was to confine all the changes to the original sanctuary area and to retain the existing furnishings. This was finally rejected on the grounds that it was attempting to plan a part of the building in isolation from the whole. If its unity was not to be obscured, the internal layout of the entire building had to be taken into account. This meant moving from a nostalgic concern for individual items of furniture to a search for the best position for the altar, the essential single focal point in any renewal worthy of the name. The basic cruciform shape of the building, and the concentration of natural light at the point where the nave and the transepts meet, decided the place for the altar beyond all doubt. The next objective was to create as much space as possible where people could be close to the altar and have the best view. The principle was accepted, not without the pain of letting go, that people at prayer take priority over obsolete furniture. The rest followed. Each of the four side chapels was given a separate sacramental function, relating them to each other and to the centre. This achieved a clearly defined theological unity and allowed the shape of the building to correspond naturally with its new range of functions. Our Lady's Shrine and the Stations of the Cross were given their own special places for the first time and not treated merely as decor. A fifteen-foot high crucifix was commissioned for the sanctuary. The Chapter Room was rearranged for small-group liturgies and exposition of the Blessed Sacrament.

The details of this work are described in these pages. The renewed interior fully meets the demands of the new liturgy without ambiguity or compromise. As a unified project, it strives to blend together a group of symbols which would convey for our time the mysteries which faith needs to express. A matter of prolonged discussion initially was whether to commission contemporary art forms and materials or to rework and reproduce existing marble pieces. As the plan became more ambitious it became clear that the scale of the proposed changes, covering the entire ground floor apart from the pews, warranted more than the craftmanship, however skilful, of repeating and reproducing forms which were in themselves pastiche. The weight of opinion came down firmly in favour of the freedom to use new designs and materials. Contemporary art by definition is more in tune with the age we live in and points more to a dynamic future than to a static past. The task, therefore, was to select and co-ordinate a team of artists with an authentic and vibrant sense of the sacred. In the cathedral, their work is enhanced by an abundance of natural light and open spaces and relates to the older building by careful conjunction with the massive stone columns, many of which are now freestanding for the first time and claiming attention in their own right. The result is a pervasive sense of calm and harmony and simplicity which is intended to create an atmosphere for prayer, an openness to the great beyond where there is eternal life and love. In the words of the psalmist: 'God is in his holy dwelling; he gives a home to the lonely, he gives power and strength to his people' (Entrance Antiphon, 17th Sunday).

Underneath the new altar lie the remains of the first four bishops of the cathedral. Their names – Charles MacNally, James Donnelly, Richard Owens and Patrick McKenna – are inscribed in Latin on a nearby wall in the south transept (see page 87). This practice of burying bishops in a crypt under the altar of their cathedral is an ancient tradition going back to the early Roman Church. In the cathedral it reminds us of our deceased founding fathers, and also that remembering the dead is at the heart of what happens at the altar. The altar is, of course, the place of the sacrifice of the cross and the table of the Lord where the people are called together to share. It is also a sign of the tomb of Christ. It tells us that his tomb is not like any other, as the women discovered when they came to anoint his dead body: 'Why look among the dead for someone who is alive?' (Luke 24:5). The piece of stone which was intended to be a tombstone, a permanent reminder of death, is now totally changed. Instead it brings everything back to life, infusing in particular the gathered assembly with the new life of the new creation. It opens beyond itself, lending symbolic approval to our profession of faith: Christ has died, Christ is risen, Christ will come again.

✠   Joseph Duffy
     Bishop of Clogher

     6 August 1998
     Feast of the Transfiguration of the Lord

1 Nave
2 South Aisle
3 North Aisle
4 Transepts
5 Altar
6 Choir
7 Chair
8 Reconciliation Room
9 Tabernacle
10 Baptismal Font
11 Aumbry
12 Lady Chapel
13 Narthex
14 Chapter Room
15 Sacristies
16 Tower Porch
17 Stations of the Cross

Ground plan of the Cathedral, drawn by Gerald MacCann

A Cathedral: A Chair-church

AUSTIN FLANNERY, OP

Look up the word cathedral in a dictionary and it may come as a surprise to learn that it is a church whose most noteworthy characteristic is that it houses a chair – or, as it is also called, a throne. There is no getting away from this description, for the very word *cathedra*, in Latin or in Greek, means chair.

But why, one might ask, is a chair the distinguishing mark of a cathedral? Is not a cathedral's altar of greater importance and relevance? Or its ambo? Or its tabernacle? And if a cathedral is so named for the chair it houses, should not every church be called a cathedral, since every church nowadays has a celebrant's chair?

The point is that the chair in a cathedral is the *bishop's* chair, one of the oldest and most important of episcopal *insignia*. It is the bishop's chair in the bishop's church. To speak of the bishop's church as a cathedral – or 'chair-church', to use a lively American expression – is to focus attention on the role of the bishop as 'true and authentic teacher of the faith' (*Decree on the Pastoral Office of Bishops in the Church, 2*). From earliest times the chair in which a bishop presides over his people was treated with respect as a symbol of his authority. For it was from his official chair that, seated facing his people, the bishop preached the gospel of Christ to them in his homilies. The chair is the symbol of the presence of the bishop; respect for the chair is respect for the bishop and for his 'sanctifying and governing' role, for his role as teacher and witness to Christ (*Decree on the Pastoral Office of Bishops in the Church*, 11, 12). The most important of all episcopal chairs has a feast in its honour, so great is the respect in which it is held: this is the chair of St Peter and the feast is on 22 February. Of course, it is not the structure which is honoured, but Peter, to whom the Lord said – the entrance antiphon of the Mass for that day reminds us – 'I have prayed that your faith may not fail; and you in your turn must strengthen your sisters and brothers.'

The Blessed Sacrament Chapel – offers a
pause, a moment of silence, an
opportunity for prayer.

The opening prayer of the Mass speaks of the Church being built 'on the rock of St Peter's confession of faith' and asks that nothing divide or weaken that 'unity in faith and love'. It is a reminder that all the episcopal chairs worldwide, all the dioceses and all the local churches form a patchwork quilt, as it were, of churches united among themselves and with the Bishop of Rome at their head.

Last January (1998) the Archbishop of Cincinnati, Daniel Pilarczyk, addressing a national meeting of cathedral pastors, recalled a question put to him during a parish meeting at which diocesan taxation had come up for discussion. A parishioner said, 'When push comes to shove, Archbishop, just what does this parish get out of being part of the archdiocese of Cincinnati?' Archbishop Pilarczyk gave credit to the Holy Spirit for the answer that, somewhat to his surprise, came from his lips: 'What do you get out of being part of the archdiocese? You get to be Catholic, and there's no other way to do it except by being connected with the church universal through the diocesan church and through the ministry of the diocesan bishop.'

Another American archbishop, John R. Roach of St Paul and Minneapolis, put it as follows:

'When we gather as a diocesan church around the bishop, we are the Church in fullness. We are Catholic. Our gathering at those moments is proclaiming a broader orthodoxy and affiliation, for we are a union of churches with the Bishop of Rome as our head.'

In the early Church and until the fourteenth century, the bishop's chair was placed in the apse, somewhat elevated so that the bishop could see and address the congregation who were at a distance from him, on the far side of the altar. From the fourteenth century

and until Vatican II, the bishop's chair, a mobile affair, tended to be placed to one side of the altar, facing across the sanctuary, no longer facing the congregation.

The liturgical reforms introduced by Vatican II have reverted to a symbolism at once more ancient and more modern. The emphasis on the bishop remains and he has been brought into sharper focus, but one which is also more inclusive, taking in as well the people whose sanctifier and teacher he is. The cathedral is seen as 'the express image of Christ's visible Church, praying, singing and worshipping on earth.'

That phrase is part of a splendid paragraph tucked away in what might seem an unlikely source, a 1965 apostolic constitution of Pope Paul VI, *Mirificus eventus*, declaring a year of jubilee. The paragraph is worth quoting in full:

The diocesan cathedral, in its architectural and artistic beauty, often stands as a splendid affirmation of our ancestors' zeal for art and religion [in Monaghan one ought to add 'and that of our contemporaries'.] It owes its dignity primarily to the fact that, as the ancient name itself signifies, it houses the *cathedra* of the bishop. The bishop's chair is like a link with the unity, order, power and truth-bearing magisterium of Peter. This is also why the cathedral church, in the splendour of its architecture, is a symbol of the spiritual temple that is built up in souls and is resplendent with the glory of divine grace. As St Paul says: 'We are the temple of the living God.' The cathedral, furthermore, should be regarded as the express image of Christ's visible Church, praying, singing and worshipping on earth. The cathedral should be regarded as the image of Christ's Mystical Body, whose members are drawn together in an organism of charity that is sustained by the outpouring of God's gifts.

The 'organism of charity' is God's people, God's family, the family of faith, which led Archbishop Pilarczyk to write, in more folksy language: 'I like to look on the cathedral as the homestead of one particular unit of the family. It's the living room and dining room where the father of the family (i.e., the bishop) sits down with the family to be family and to do what the family does together.'

And it led Archbishop Roach to say: 'The cathedral is part of the life, faith and worship of the people of my diocese. It is their home and it is the place where I invite them to join at the Lord's table.'

But what of the (increasing?) number of Irish Catholics who remain Catholic only in the sense that it is the Catholic church which they no longer attend? And what of those for whom even that measure of association is too much? Does the 'architectural and artistic beauty' of a cathedral have anything to say to them?

Mario Botta, the architect of France's newest cathedral, believes that it has much to say to them. His highly-esteemed modern cylindrical cathedral in Evry, a new town about sixty miles from Paris, opened for worship in 1995 and was consecrated in 1997. The Catholic Church in France has shed far, far more members in recent centuries than has the Catholic Church in Ireland to date. It is not much more than forty years since a leading French intellectual proclaimed that France was a pagan country. It has far more unbelievers than believers. Yet Botta wrote:

A cathedral, nowadays, affords an extraordinary opportunity for constructing and enriching a living space. It is a new sign for the people. It offers a pause, a moment of silence, an opportunity for prayer, which speaks to us of a humanity confronting rapid changes and the contradictions of modern life.

The bishop's chair in the bishop's church

Yes, I believe that a cathedral is needed by unbelievers as well as by believers. It links us with our glorious past. To build a cathedral is not just to build the bishop's church. It is above all to assert that the powers which are most truly real are still present.

Later, he added that a cathedral 'takes us back through a thousand years of history and fills the empty spaces in the memory of a modern town. If we are to link our epoch to historic memory we need more than institutions designed to meet the city's daily "functional" needs. We also need structures capable of linking the men and women of today to the riches and memory of a heritage, a collective patrimony.'

A Cathedral of its time

AMBROSE MACAULAY

THE MENTION of the word 'cathedral' usually conjures up the image of the great medieval Gothic buildings which adorn several European countries. One tends to think of Chartres, York Minster or Cologne. Its size, style and beauty, however, do not define a cathedral: what does define it is service as the bishop's church from which he communicates the gospel to his people. The splendid Gothic cathedrals of Europe belong to the middle ages and their magnificence was often dictated by local pride and the desire of princes, cities or kingdoms to outshine one another. An entirely different set of circumstances governed the origin, size and adornments of the great majority of the Catholic cathedrals of Ireland which were built in the nineteenth century.

By the middle of the eighteenth century, Irish bishops felt free to reside in their sees. Though these maintained their pre-Reformation names and boundaries, the bishops did not generally attempt to take up residence beside the ancient cathedral, which was then in the possession of the Church of Ireland, or in the village or town which gave its name to the diocese. In most cases they chose to live where a fairly large number of Catholics were to be found or, where they had a choice in that respect, in a place where they could find a house. Some moved from town to town until the early decades of the nineteenth century.

The archbishops of Armagh lived at Drogheda until the 1830s. The town of Armagh and the surrounding district were substantially Protestant; Drogheda and Louth were much more Catholic and offered a more hospitable home. Until 1825 the bishops of Down and Connor lived in or near Downpatrick; the barony of Lecale in Co Down contained, perhaps, more Catholics than any other part of the diocese and bishops found the atmosphere there more congenial. In other dioceses as, for example, in Kerry,

Kildare and Leighlin or Ardagh, the bishops lived in various parishes before choosing the growing or central town of the diocese as the centre of diocesan administration and the site of the cathedral.

The diocese of Clogher shared this experience. Daniel and Hugh O'Reilly, who were bishops from 1747 to 1801 lived at Carrickmacross. James Murphy, who was bishop from 1801 to 1824, lived in the parish of Tydavnet. His coadjutor and successor, Edward Kernan, lived in Carrickmacross. Charles MacNally, who became coadjutor in 1843, went to live in the parish of Clogher and remained there after his succession to the see. In 1851, on the death of the parish priest of Monaghan, he took over that parish and moved his residence to the town. Already the diocesan college had been opened in Monaghan; with the bishop's move Monaghan became the diocesan capital. MacNally, like his brethren elsewhere in Ireland, judged that it would be a large flourishing town and, situated on the crossing of main thoroughfares, was the most suitable place for his diocesan headquarters. The next step was the provision of a cathedral.

In the twentieth century, cathedrals like those of Galway and Liverpool, which were dedicated in the 1960s, were built as a proclamation of God's presence, a statement of faith to their city communities and, perhaps, also to highlight the importance of the dioceses. They were not strictly necessary for the pastoral well-being of the Catholic people. In both places there were smaller churches serving as pro-cathedrals and a sufficient number of other churches to serve the needs of the people.

The cathedrals of nineteenth century Ireland had a very different origin. Their immediate purpose was practical. They were required for their congregations for Sunday and daily worship and in most cases they replaced the poor chapels which had served

*Carrara marble figures in the arcade on the south
transept gable (see page 72)*

preceding generations but which were usually too small or decrepit to permit of further development. The chapels built in the late eighteenth or early nineteenth century all over Ireland were being knocked down and new, solid and substantial and, it was hoped, lasting buildings were being put up in their place. Church building in the cathedral towns was generally little different from that in other towns. The pastoral care of the people required better churches, and the difference between the new cathedrals and the churches of the larger parishes was not enormous. The cathedrals were larger and better furnished, but their use and the services they provided were little different from those in all other parish churches.

It was no accident that much of this cathedral building took place in the second quarter of the nineteenth century, though it often continued into the third quarter. The chapels in towns like Tuam, Newry, Carlow, Ballina, Ennis and Skibbereen were in poor shape by 1825. The bishops decided that it was time not only to replace them but to do so with structures of greater solidity and dignity which, as cathedrals, could be enlarged, enriched and paid for over the course of the following decades. Waterford and Dublin had already led the way; their cathedral and pro-cathedral were opened in 1796 and 1825 respectively. In 1840 the foundation stones of St Patrick's in Armagh and St Mel's in Longford were laid. Before the Famine, which caused work on these cathedrals to be discontinued, others were begun at Enniscorthy, Killarney and Kilkenny.

The great problem facing the bishops of Ireland was finance. The Catholic population was for the most part, not only poor, but also increasing rapidly. Throughout the country priests were everywhere looking for funds to build churches, schools and in some cases diocesan colleges. It was as if too many fishermen were fishing in the same

*The Cathedral – undisputed eminence among
the buildings of the town and countryside*

lake. Some solved the problem partly by appealing to emigrants in Britain and America, but the Irish abroad had local calls on their charity and often little superfluous cash to give away.

The diocese of Clogher was somewhat slower to undertake the construction of a cathedral than its neighbours in Armagh, Dromore, Ardagh and Derry. The Irish Catholic Directory of 1843 gave part of the explanation:

> Clogher has felt the impulse of the times, and continues to emulate her most active neighbours in the race of virtue and improvement ... Large and commodious churches are to be seen almost in every parish. A splendid seminary is erected at Monaghan, in the centre of the diocese.

Local circumstances accounted for part of the delay. The parish of Monaghan did not become vacant till 1851 and so it was only then that Bishop MacNally could take it over as a mensal and make it available for such a project. Ten years later the foundation stone of a neo-Gothic structure designed by J. J. McCarthy, the 'Irish Pugin', was laid.

And it is to Augustus Welby Pugin (1812-52) that the neo-Gothic designs of most of the Irish cathedrals of the nineteenth century are due. The Romantics of the early nineteenth century extolled the virtues and the beauty of medieval Christianity and its expression in Gothic art. Pugin popularised the style in Britain and it was he who designed the cathedrals at Enniscorthy and Killarney. He succeeded in reawakening a pride in the architecture of 'the ages of faith', and convincing Catholics in Britain and Ireland, who were then bent on 'restoring' their church, that neo-Gothic was somehow the supremely Catholic style.

It was no surprise that Bishop MacNally chose Pugin's Irish follower as his architect.

An Example of the Gothic style in Ireland

MILDRED DUNNE

THE REVIVAL of Gothic in Ireland goes back to the eighteenth century, when it made its appearance in the 'Gothick' castles which were thought appropriate for the romantic wildness of the Irish landscape. It was subsequently taken up for ecclesiastical use by the Established Church, which adopted a late Gothic style – the Perpendicular – which it applied to box-shaped churches, many of which had western towers. The Perpendicular Gothic style was prevalent in English architecture from the middle of the fourteenth up to the sixteenth century. The Irish Gothick of the pre-Famine years was a superficial attempt to build in the Gothic idiom. Maurice Craig has described it 'as a semi-serious carpenter's Gothick' which bore little resemblance to the Gothic architecture of the middle ages.

By the 1820s, when the church began to turn to Gothic, the Perpendicular style still in fashion, architects felt that the Perpendicular style was the acme of Gothic architecture. In the first half of the nineteenth century in Dublin, Gothic was almost exclusively an ecclesiastical style. Outside Dublin, the beginnings of St Patrick's Cathedral in Armagh, Thomas A. Cobden's Cathedral of the Assumption at Carlow, built c.1820, and Dominic Madden's cathedral at Tuam, built 1827, have in common this late Gothic style, incorporating a classically symmetrical design embellished with spiky ornament and plaster decoration.

Towards the middle of the nineteenth century, architects under the influence of the ecclesiologists and A.W.N. Pugin enunciated a different, more serious and archaeologically 'correct' Gothic architecture. They preferred the earlier Gothic styles, Early English or Decorated, the Gothic of the thirteenth and fourteenth centuries, and began to look to continental Gothic. Their attitude to planning was functional – the parts of a church and their location should be dictated by liturgical requirements. Ornament had to be of natural materials and related to the essential construction. A material such as plaster was considered a 'sham' – if the building was to look like stone, it ought to built of stone. This produced a sturdy, picturesque, more archaeologically-motivated style, found in Pugin's own churches in Ireland in the 1840s.

The choosing of the correct medieval Gothic involved more than just architectural taste. The Catholic and Church of Ireland Churches were anxious to establish continuity with the Christian Church in what was considered to be its finest period – that of the building of Chartres and Reims, and of Lincoln and Exeter. Indeed for Irish Catholics there was a strong element of self affirmation. This affirmation was implicit in building Gothic stone churches with soaring spires in towns and villages where medieval buildings were either in ruins or had been taken over by the Established Church. The idea of religious revival in the Catholic Church was very much bound up, in the 1840s, with the idea of a return to a more perfect Celtic past. The medieval period was seen as a golden age and the temptation to recreate it was great among Irish Catholics, for whom it would hark back to, and indeed herald, an era of religious freedom.

The building of St Macartan's Cathedral

Many towns in Ireland witnessed the enormous efforts made by the Irish Catholics at home and abroad to replace the churches and cathedrals which had remained in ruins since the Reformation and to build grander edifices than had been common in the Penal period. The building programme of the Catholic Church in Ireland had been

The Cathedral of St Mac Carthain, Monaghan, Ireland — Mr J. J. McCarthy, Architect.
The Builder, *September 12, 1868*

gathering momentum since Catholic Emancipation in 1829. By the 1850s, Derry, Enniscorthy and Killarney cathedrals were under construction or completed, and a need was seen by the Catholics in Monaghan for a cathedral. With these sentiments, the story of St Macartan's Cathedral unfolds. On 3 January 1858, at a meeting of the Catholics of Monaghan, with Bishop MacNally presiding, it was formally resolved that a new church at Monaghan was necessary. The diocese of Clogher, according to Bishop Mac Nally, had 'no cathedral church, nor even cathedral services, properly speaking'. An eight-acre site was purchased by the bishop from Humphrey Jones of Clontibret for £800, and the architect, James Joseph McCarthy of Dublin, was employed to draw up a design. On 21 June 1861, the foundation stone was solemnly laid in the presence of the bishops of Ireland. By April 1862, the work was under way. By August of that year the foundations were complete 'and the massive arches below the surface show that they were intended to bear an enormous weight'. It was not long after, however, that the bishop began to experience some difficulties with his building programme.

J. J. McCarthy – 'the Irish Pugin'

The beginning of J. J. McCarthy's career had coincided with the upsurge in church building between 1850 and 1880. His considerable output of churches and ecclesiastical works had much to do with the evolution of the Gothic style which became standard in Catholic church building during this period. McCarthy had completed the cathedral in Killarney, making that town the ecclesiastical envy of all. This Gothic style was to give the emerging Catholic population a visual identity which would last for the rest of the century. Often referred to as 'the Irish Pugin', J. J. McCarthy claimed friendship with

The Cathedral of St Mac Carthain, Monaghan, Ireland — plan.
The Builder, *September* 12, 1868

A. W. N. Pugin, and was certainly his most fervent disciple in Ireland. He was born in Dublin in 1817 of parents from County Kerry. His death in 1882 saw him leave behind an architectural legacy which was continued during the rest of the century. Although many of his ideas came from Pugin, he evolved a personal style following ecclesiological principles, and taking local conditions into account. Fully imbued with this ecclesiological outlook, J. J. McCarthy proceeded with his architectural career. Pugin's ideas about Gothic architecture included the proper design and decoration of churches, which he promoted with great determination at the time when ecclesiastical architecture in Ireland was about to enter quite a prolific period.

I am building a cathedral in the native town of a friend of mine (one C. G. D.) and when you see it if you say that I have not fufilled my friend's promise of twenty golden years ago, I will hang myself.

So wrote McCarthy in a letter to Charles Gavan Duffy, dated 19 April 1865.

Lord Rossmore and the quarry controversy

In 1866, the local landowner, Lord Rossmore, offered the use of the stone from the Tirkeenan quarry until 1871. This local Monaghan stone is a hard grey- and cream-coloured limestone which came from the quarry near Old Cross Square, beyond the former gasworks. There was no charge for the stone, but when finished, the holes were to be filled in by the bishop or by Rossmore's men at the bishop's expense. This agreement appeared to be a good start to the building programme. According to an account dating from 1864 in the *Freeman's Journal*

… it was not unusual to see 400 or 500 horses and carts, filled with lime, stone and

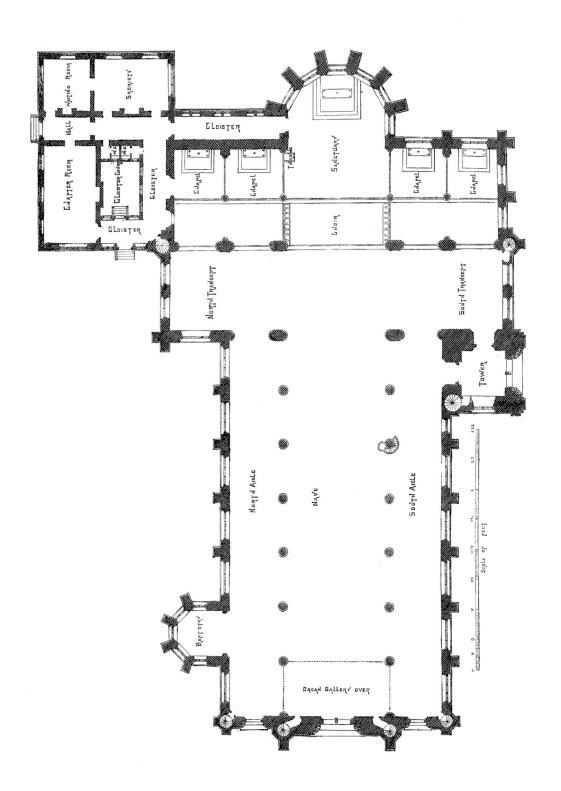

sand, arrive at the building together; the horses and carts and men having being supplied gratuitously by the people of the various parishes surrounding.

Bishop Donnelly quarried extensively until 1877, when solicitors for Lord Rossmore stated that the terms of the 1866 agreement were not being carried out. The cathedral was at this stage far from completion. Bishop Donnelly, writing to Lord Rossmore's solicitor Mr Wright, stated that 'the Roman Catholics of Monaghan would be grateful for the use of the quarry for even one year longer'. He thought that 'this would be sufficient; but if this [could not] be conceded, [he would] proceed as soon as the season permits such a work, to fill in the quarry hole and deliver up the premises with sincerest gratitude for the prolonged use of the same'. Another year's use was granted at the end of 1877, but the bishop thought it impossible to fill up the hole and by August of 1878, Lord Rossmore had insisted on the immediate filling of the hole. By October a legal notice was issued on behalf of Rossmore to Donnelly from Wright, insisting that he comply with the contract of 1866. Donnelly's counsel, John O'Hagan, advised him to fill up the quarried hole and if this was impossible to offer full value of the fee-simple. An agreement was reached in November 1878 with Bishop Donnelly accepting Lord Rossmore's offer of a further two years of quarrying.

By 1886, eight years later, there was a surplus of 3,000 tons of stone. Donnelly decided to sell them to Connolly, the contractor for the local asylum which was under construction at the time. Wright expressed Rossmore's anger at the stones being used for other purposes and explicitly stated that 'No more stones [are] to be quarried until those already raised are used up; all stones are to be *for the Cathedral* purpose only.' The negotiations continued until the 1890s, with the bishop relenting and agreeing to pay

£250 for a fee-simple value of the land quarried. He maintained that he would never be able to pay for the land to be filled in which he estimated would cost £2000. Bishop Donnelly was dissatisfied with the end result, and continued to harbour a grievance against Rossmore's behaviour in the complicated negotiations. The bishop knew that the real source of hostility between Rossmore and himself was not the quarry but the long and bitter tenant right agitation of the period in which both men were actively and prominently involved.

The style of St Macartan's Cathedral

As the Gothic revival movement coincided with Catholic Emancipation in Ireland, there was a need to find symbols to express publicly Catholic worship. The outstanding style to be chosen was one which could be recreated in a manner that was truthful to the principles expounded by A. W. N. Pugin. McCarthy chose Decorated for important buildings like the cathedrals at Monaghan and Armagh. The name Decorated was traditionally applied to English Gothic of c. 1300-1350, although it can now be applied to the majority of European church projects of this period, with their complex and varied ornament. The main features of the style are obvious from the outside of St Macartan's: the large rose and lancet windows adorned with elaborate tracery; the pointed arches and doors; the numerous turrets and pinnacles; and the thick, stepped buttresses separating the bays, particularly of the apse and Lady Chapel. Monaghan Cathedral's characteristics of French Gothic, as opposed to English, are the far greater emphasis on height and the polygonal form of the apse or 'chevet'; in medieval English architecture a square eastern termination was preferred. The interior is a combination of both the

The sanctuary before the present renovation

English and the French characteristics – the hammerbeam roof is English and the piers and capitals are French.

The site chosen for the cathedral eminently suited a Gothic structure. As affirmation of Roman Catholic resurgence, Armagh and Monaghan cathedrals were required to be impressive buildings with plenty of opportunity for display. St Patrick's Cathedral at Armagh was restarted in 1851 by McCarthy in a 'Puginian, rather French, Decorated' style, as noted by Jeanne Sheehy, having been initially begun in 1840 by Thomas Duff in the English Perpendicular style. St Macartan's Cathedral is situated on a hill at some distance from the town centre, with an attractive approach up the hillside by flights of stone steps, laid out and landscaped in 1948. Monaghan Cathedral dominates its environment. The grounds of the cathedral are spacious, allowing it to be viewed from all angles. With its single southern tower and spire, perhaps less striking than the twin towers at Armagh, it is more coherent, having being conceived and built entirely in the Decorated style. It is an example of a rather muscular High Victorian Gothic, a style McCarthy used for other important town churches, for example at SS. Peter and Paul's at Kilmallock, Co Limerick and St Patrick's, Dungannon, Co Tyrone.

The muscularity of the cathedral is achieved in various ways: by placing important windows in recessed panels; by situating buttresses at right angles to each other at corners, then emphasising them with a pinnacle or turret; by marking the bays of the apse or aisles with stepped buttresses; and by using roughly dressed stone for walls. The choice of style may have been due to personal preference, but it could also be attributed to pressure from McCarthy's clients. The Church, which had at last funds to plan and carry through large building projects, felt that the simpler forms of medieval architec-

The magnificent hammerbeam roof with projecting angel terminals

ture were not striking enough for the later nineteenth-century taste. Pugin had used the earlier forms of Gothic, the Early English style, in the Cathedral of St Mary's in Killarney which dates from 1842, and McCarthy had used the style for many of his smaller rural churches. The taste in the mid-nineteenth century was for a far more ornate and yet restrained architecture, as exemplified in the work of McCarthy and of his successor at Monaghan, William Hague.

William Hague and the building of the spire

Before McCarthy's death on 6 February 1882, he had lived to see the skeleton of his magnificent edifice – with the walls and roof completed. His successor was the Cavan architect William Hague, who was responsible for the erection of the spire and the gate lodge. In carrying out McCarthy's design for the spire, Hague has been credited with the 'the good sense and artistic honesty to avoid introducing his own personality at the expense of symmetry and unity' *(A History of St Macartan's Cathedral and its Patron Saint*, 1949, p. 50). McCarthy's initial perspective and plan (see page 31) appeared in *The Builder* of 1868. As illustrated, the nave is longer by two bays and there is a view of the tower with a spire. Comparisons between this perspective and the spire as built re-inforce the notion that Hague did not slavishly imitate McCarthy's design. The angle turrets appear more pronounced and inventive as opposed to the more linear and elong-ated design of McCarthy from 1868. One of McCarthy's original architectural drawings, however, shows a pyramidal termination to the square tower. McCarthy evidently intended to build a spire at a later stage as the drawing is titled 'Temporary Roof on Tower'.

The tower and spire adjoin the south transept, a feature employed in many of

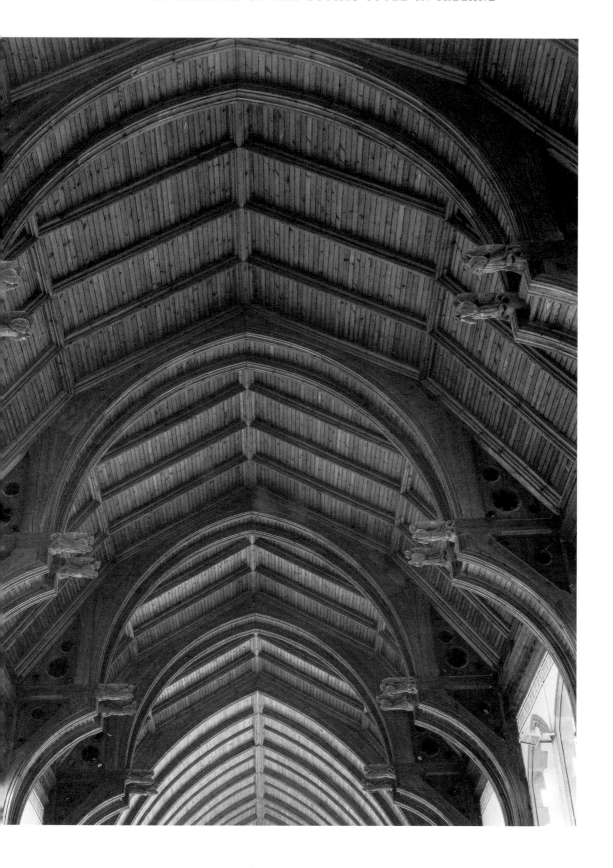

McCarthy's churches. At the springing of the spire in a cluster of detail, a marked contrast is achieved between the relative severity and simplicity of the tower and the ornate qualities of the spire (see page 95). The lateral turrets at the broached corners at the base of the spire are daring in both conception and execution. The detailed handling of these turrets is not in keeping with the design detail elsewhere in the cathedral. This is an indication of Hague's influence on the final design of the spire. There are almost unbroken buttresses from the base of the tower to the corbel table which is just below the tower's two two-light windows. This 'bold verticality of treatment' was identified by the *Dublin Builder* in 1865 as the cathedral's leading characteristic throughout.

During the building of the spire complications arose. Hague employed three brothers to erect the spire – John, Arthur and Bernard McElhatton. The contractors were to use the stone in the Bloomhill Quarry in Dungannon. The contract was signed in March 1883, allowing for the sum of £2204 9s 2d to be spent on the spire. By September of that year, John McElhatton wrote to the bishop of his going into the bankruptcy court and suggested his brothers would finish the work. Mr Dooley, the clerk of works, was in regular communication with Hague, and informed him of situations that arose. At the start of October, Donnelly wired Hague that work at the cathedral was not going satisfactorily. Hague replied that the spire was '44 feet high' and 'at the comparatively plain portion'. He hoped that McElhatton would finish without interruption.

Yet by the end of October 1883 Hague wrote to the bishop saying that Dooley had informed him that the McElhattons were 'violating the specification' in the way they were pointing the stone. He informed the bishop that they were 'carrying up the spire in an irregular manner and of unequal sides instead of having the four faces alike'. Problems arose relating to the leaking of the windows, the difficulty of getting the required supply of blue slates, and the storms with 'terrible damage done to the cathedral'. A second storm was predicted, while

'not a hand [has been] put to it by the contractors – even the heavy beam hanging from the top of the scaffold over cathedral roof and ready to fall and sure to cut through the cathedral roof [was] not touched'.

Hague would not tolerate the further delays and wrote to the McElhattons:

Finding the Roman cathedral of Monaghan left derelict by the roofs and spire in danger of being wrecked and a probability of loss of life and property from your neglect and breach of contract I shall proceed...to have such salvage proceedings taken...

A legal notice was served on the same day to the McElhattons. The following day, 31 January 1884, John McElhatton maintained that 'the accident with the top stone is the cause of all these delays latterly'. With the apology of the contractors for their failure in the contract, the spire was finished at the end of 1884. The problems with the spire, however, continued up to the 1970s, with the proposal to remove the turrets in 1976 due to structural problems.

Purdy and Millard and the splendour of the interior space

The basic structure of the cathedral is cruciform, with two lateral transepts, a nave and two side aisles. The typical features of the Gothic style appear in the interior – the pointed arches, the foliated carving of the capitals and the carved heads on the corbel stones supporting the roof. One must, however, look behind the medievalism to appre-

Cararra marble figures in the arcade on the gable of the
north transept (see page 73)

ciate the true interior space. In October 1873 the working drawings for the roof were
almost complete and also the details for the tower windows. By March of 1875 the roof
was still incomplete. The work for the walls and the roof were done by direct labour,
whereas the remaining work was contracted out. McCarthy uses the hammerbeam as
the roof structure for the cathedral (see page 37). It consists of simple timber laths with
little or no decoration, supported by twelve pairs of carved angel terminals which appear
to hold the roof aloft. The timber laths and purlins are supported by the transverse arches
of the hammerbeam structure. These arches are carried down on paired slim timber
colonettes to corbelled heads. The firm, Purdy and Millard, were employed in May 1878
on a two-tier contract for the execution of the woodwork of the roof and then the
stonework of the capitals and columns. The hammerbeam angels cost £1 each.

The hammerbeam roof does not appear to be typical of the Gothic revivalists' choice
for roof structure. It appears as a rather weighty alternative to the open trussed timber
roof or the variations on timber panelled roofs. The hammerbeam was perhaps a more
interesting roof structure, and was employed by A.W.N. Pugin. Yet contemporary
churches show that architects preferred the more delicate scissor truss roof. In England
during this period some hammerbeams were built, but generally they were confined to
chancels, being appropriate to the square-ended English usage. The simple ribbing of
the chancel roof in Monaghan distinguishes it from the hammerbeam treatment in the
nave. The two-fold division and treatment of nave and chancel decoratively are indicative
of the Church Militant and the Church Triumphant – those of an earthly and a heavenly
disposition. The side aisles and four side chapels are considerably lower than the nave,
transepts and chancel, an indication of their secondary role in the overall structure.

The first view of the interior from the west entrance reveals, more clearly than is seen from the exterior, the basic cruciform plan of the building, and focuses naturally on the altar at the crossing. The reworking of the cathedral, conceived in the Gothic style for the Tridentine liturgy, to serve the liturgy as reformed by Vatican II, was performed by Michael Biggs and the architect, Gerald MacCann, from 1983 to 1986. One becomes aware of the unexpected spaciousness, only fully revealed since the re-ordering of the sanctuary space. The altar was moved forward to beneath the crossing, where the transepts meet the nave and the chancel, to allow for the maximum participation in the Eucharist. The bishop's chair or *cathedra* occupies the central place at the back of the apse and is surrounded by a semi-circular presbyterium for concelebrants. The main floor level in the chancel was raised six steps higher than the nave floor, with the presbyterium raised two steps further. The altar area in polished travertine is now the focal point of the cathedral and has a definite air of dominance. The new sanctuary is open and flows easily to the floor of the nave. The four side chapels have also been rearranged with the removal of altar rails and cast-iron grilles which divided them in half. One can now appreciate their full architectural depth. With the removal of the pulpit a clear visual line has been created from the west door to the apse. The essential function of the original plan of the nineteenth-century interior has, therefore, been maintained while facing the renewed challenges of the twentieth century.

McCarthy's standard form of nave arcade consists of chamfered pointed arches resting on plain circular columns set on octagonal bases and terminating in foliated capitals. The individual detail of the capitals was not left to the masons and sculptors as was often the practice in churches at this time. McCarthy, while he was unable to make it to Monaghan, placed his son Charles in charge of the interior decoration. Charles McCarthy had orders to make the firm do a trial capital as specified by McCarthy in order to find out their potential in copying the design sent by him. The capitals appear to exhibit an earlier style of decoration than is displayed in the rest of the church. They follow a two-tier stylised acanthus arrangement which was a much stiffer style than the more natural foliated capitals being sculpted at this time. Such an arrangement was often used in French Romanesque churches in the Provence region.

Conclusion

Monaghan Cathedral has not only aisles but transepts, not only sacristies but a chapter house, not only a tower and spire, but a striking baptistery, which is now part of the sanctuary. It remains one of the most impressive cathedrals built in the Gothic revival period. It remains true to its function and to McCarthy's promise to Charles Gavan Duffy of 'twenty golden years ago'.

The Cathedral Renewed

LOUIS MCREDMOND

EXTENSIVE CHANGES were made in St Macartan's Cathedral, Monaghan, to adapt it to the needs of the modern liturgy. The result is a reconstruction totally suited to its purpose while consciously respecting the lines and spirit of the old building. Few adaptations have been undertaken on such a scale with such success.

The cathedral church of the Ulster borderland diocese of Clogher stands on a hill outside the market town of Monaghan in the Republic of Ireland. A better-than-average example of Victorian Gothic, it looks more French than English, being many-gabled with an apse, a stumpy spire and serried ranks of very Latin saints gesticulating, haranguing and beseeching heaven from their niches. Inside, the sanctuary area used to encompass not only the high altar in the apse at the east end, but two side-chapels against the east wall of each transept. A long railing, bisecting the transepts and cutting across the top of the nave, sharply separated this area of liturgical action from the laity, who were clearly envisaged as the prayerful spectators of sacred ritual.

In 1982 Bishop Joseph Duffy and Mr Gerald MacCann, architect to the cathedral, called in the Dublin sculptor, the late Michael Biggs, to help them adapt this interior to the needs of the post-conciliar liturgical renewal. There were Roman regulations to be met. The involvement of the laity in a single worshipping community had to be emphasised. So also had the special ministries of priest and bishop. It was desirable to avoid any appearance of contradiction between the new arrangements and the old building, designed for a different age. Since the greater part of the project concerned the design, carving and placement of furnishings, the key role fell to the sculptor, subject to the advice, encouragement and cautions of the bishop and the architect.

Michael Biggs began with the altar. It had to be brought out of 'the clerical area', he

The breath-taking huge sweep of the renewed sanctuary area

decided, and be set down 'among the people'. In a cruciform Gothic church the only place *dictated by the building itself* where this objective could be met was the crossing where the transepts joined the nave. The decision to place the altar in the crossing at once determined that other decisions would have to be made. The railing was already doomed but, in addition, all existing altars – high altar and side-chapels – had to go as well. An altar as central and as unifying as Biggs proposed could not be expected to compete with rival focal points. Not only were the distractions removed, but the new and only altar was made to declaim its own significance. The sculptor chiselled it from a block of Dublin mountain granite, stippling its outward-facing surfaces for relief but otherwise giving it no decoration. He rounded its corners to soften them and chipped a gentle inward curve where it touched the floor – enough to suggest the table of the supper without diminishing the altar of sacrifice. Raised up at the point where the lines of nave and transepts and apse converge, this grey-white monolith, sturdy, plain and pleasing, dominates the church from every angle, as if to say 'I am what this building is about'.

With the pews of the transepts facing one another from either side of the altar, and with those of the nave facing it in front, the unifying effect is dramatically stated. The high recess of the apse remains. It could have been redundant space. Instead it is made the natural home for a 'clerical area'. At the innermost point of the apse Biggs put the *cathedra*, the bishop's chair ... and chair it is, not throne, but undoubtedly the *locus* of authority. Here the magistrate would have presided in the ancient Roman basilicas, the remote ancestors of this type of building. The 'magistrate' in Monaghan, however, is not left in lonely eminence. The chair, of similar granite and finish as the altar, has curving benches to its right and left, seats for the senior clergy in lieu of stalls, the whole ensemble

both symbolising and actually presenting the bishop in the midst of his priests. The curving benches neatly tuck into the angled 'curve' of the apse. The integrity of the building is therefore not disturbed and the apsidal area is used for an appropriate purpose. The space between *cathedra* and altar is partly occupied by another chair (for the celebrant at Mass) and the *ambo* or reading-desk, each repeating the now familiar granite finish.

Much space is left unfilled, nonetheless, and it would take a more expert commentator than I to explain why this looks absolutely right: it has to do with the relationship of volume to space, of the solid chunks of granite to the cubic capacity of the part of the church in which they stand. The floor, too, plays an integral role in pleasing the eye. Done throughout in travertine – a limestone of the palest pink – widely-spaced shallow steps lift up the altar for all to see. Behind it, another step edges the ambo just a little higher, while the *cathedra* and stall-benches in their turn are raised up further. Biggs in this way contrives a foreshortening of the whole area so that a worshipper in the nave feels reasonably close to even the distant *cathedra*. By thus underscoring the oneness of God's people, by drawing them together, architecture gives physical expression to contemporary theology.

Travertine proliferates, spilling over to form the floor of the former side-chapels and to cover the walls where their altars used to stand. It serves as cladding on the wall of the apse behind the stall-benches up to window level. Ranging out behind and beneath the new furnishings, it implies a warm embrace and an invitation to involvement by contrast with the railings of the past which divided the church – both building and people – into primary and secondary segments. The invitation is not only to come to the altar.

The four side chapels accommodate a variety of features essential or appropriate to a Catholic church. In the right-hand side chapel, next to the sanctuary, the tabernacle of gleaming silver-gilt (by Richard King) rests atop a tall Biggs-carved granite plinth. A baptismal font occupies the corresponding space in the other transept, a great shallow basin (of granite, naturally!) shaped as a cushioned square set diagonally on another cushion-shape to hint at the traditional octagon of a font without actually reproducing it – which might have clashed with the softly-rounded corners of the other granite fittings.

To the left of the font, in the travertined wall, is an *aumbry*, a recess behind a grill for storing the jars of oil employed in various ceremonies such as Confirmation and Anointing the sick. On the far side, beyond the tabernacle in the facing other side chapel, is the one element of the reconstruction which troubles me: a confessional in the beehive form of a Celtic monastic cell. It suitably replaces the old 'confession boxes' (all of which have been removed) since it is really a place of one-to-one welcome in the general ambience of all the sacramental symbols. Aesthetically, however, a building within a building rarely looks right. Even the lovely chantry chapels, found in large English churches, can seem architecturally tautological. They say, in effect, 'this space has nothing to do with what goes on out there'.

The Monaghan reconstruction would be bland enough, almost two-dimensional, if it consisted solely of travertine and granite. The Victorian glass of the windows sheds some light but little colour. If a ghostly quality, creating an atmosphere of mystery in altogether the wrong sense, was to be avoided, a note of opulence had somehow to be struck to set off the chaste pallidity. The solution was found in tapestry, a material and an art form highly developed in Ireland today although normally featured in church

The multi-coloured tapestry behind the cathedra, depicting (left to right) the legend of St Macartan, the Blessed Trinity, and the Annunciation to Joseph

only as as an altar frontal or a decorative hanging on a lectern. For Michael Biggs it was a particularly satisfying decision since it enabled him to draw on the talents of his wife.

Frances Biggs is a renaissance woman of myriad accomplishments: she has been a violinist in the national symphony orchestra and is a painter, superb stained glass artist … and tapestry designer. For Monaghan, she designed five tapestries, three to hang behind the *cathedra*, the others behind the font and the tabernacle respectively. The voluptuous blues and reds, the greens and crumbling whites of these great carpet-banners are trumpet voluntaries of colour, filling the travertined paleness with vibrant exultation. They perfectly complement the hardness of stone and the ordered restraint of the rest of the concept. They are quite stunning. They tell stories, too. The Holy Spirit descends upon the water at the font. The fractured host of the Eucharist backs the tabernacle. The legend of Saint Macartan, disciple of Saint Patrick and founder of the diocese, the circle of the Trinity, and the Annunciation to Joseph, are depicted behind the chair. But the first and last message remains the colour, rich in itself and deep with the plushness of wool.

The tapestries are *vital* to the scheme, which is to say life-giving. In that, they capture the profundity of all that has been done at Monaghan, the repeated assertion of sacrament, of God-with-us. In themselves and in what they illuminate, they show us the sense in which we can truly speak of *sacred art*.

The Cathedral Artists:
A Release of Creative Energy

ELTIN GRIFFIN O.CARM

'We like you as bishop, I hope you like us as artists.'

S o wrote Frances Biggs in her innocence on behalf of herself and her husband
Michael at the early stages of their acquaintance with Bishop Joseph Duffy of
the diocese of Clogher, who commissioned both of them to undertake the major
part of the art work in the re-ordering of the cathedral. Such a tentative expression of
trust was to blossom into a mature friendship across the years. From day one, Frances
won the respect of the bishop by insisting that the Blessed Sacrament area should take
the shape of a contemplative space and should not be encumbered by any conventional
ecclesiastical bric-à-brac. Her recommendation paid off. The place of reservation, which
relates to the ancient tradition of reserving the Blessed Sacrament when Mass is over, is
literally a pool of quiet in a very large building.

Frances Biggs

To return to Frances Biggs, her involvement with the RTÉ Symphony Orchestra as
a violinist for forty years is mentioned elsewhere in this volume. Music is a predominant
motif in all her work, especially in the cathedral, visual music.

Her artistic work is manifold. It includes hundreds of paintings, stained glass and
tapestry, which is her great love. Gonzaga College Chapel in Dublin is quintessential
Frances Biggs. Her brilliant stained glass covers what seem to be literally acres of wall.
The Stations of the Cross at Renmore, in her native city of Galway, represent her early
work. The Apocalypse tapestry behind the altar in the Church of the Resurrection,
Killarney, is a very striking piece of work despite its lack of proportion to the entire edifice.

Funds were not available for a larger piece. Terenure College in Dublin commissioned her for eight stained glass windows of Carmelite saints and beati. The window of Blessed Titus Brandsma, who died in the concentration camp at Dachau in 1942, is the chief feature in the Chapel of the Martyrs. Michael Biggs crafted the exquisite lettering on the stone table in the same chapel, bearing the names of eleven contemporary martyrs.

The tapestries in the cathedral, which are the joint work of Frances Biggs and weaver Terry Dunne, must be among the foremost of modern tapestries, with their incredible merging and mixing of strikingly beautiful colours. In more recent times, a tapestry of the Trinity has been added in a captivating design. Across the centuries, different images and metaphors have been used to depict the Triune God such as source, river, stream, or Lover, Beloved, Love. Frances manages to capture the all-embracing love of the Father, reaching down to the humanity of the Son and to the power and omnipresence of the Holy Spirit. Back to the music again, the entire portrayal of the Trinity is like a musical chord in harmony.

Vestments

In the cathedral vestments Frances captured something else. That the beauty of a vestment should derive from its material and form, rather than from ornamentation, is the directive given in the Irish Pastoral Directory on the Building and Re-ordering of Churches (*The Place of Worship*, Veritas, The Institute of Pastoral Liturgy 1994). The form and cut of vestments should be designed in such a way that they harmonise with the ambience of the particular church in which they are used. The final rejoinder is that they should be entrusted to a competent artist. The competent artist for Monaghan was

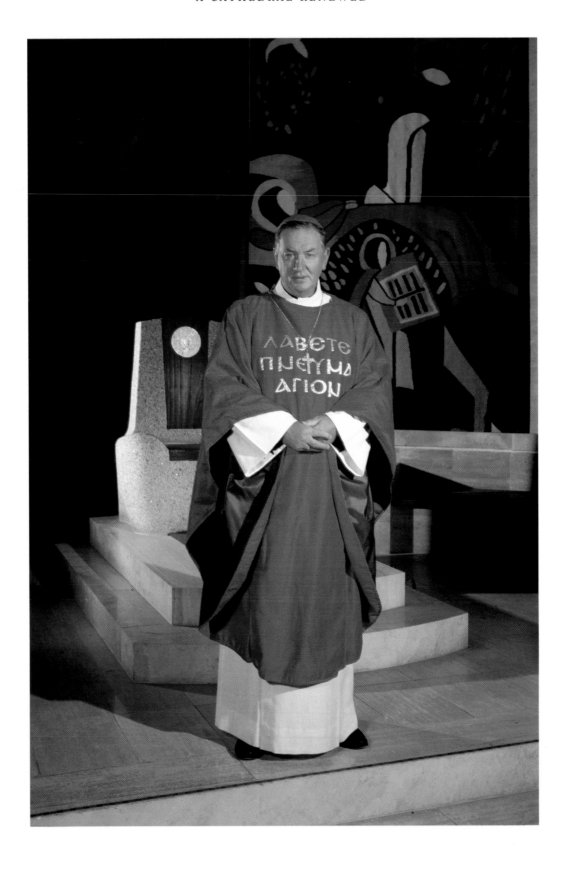

The vestments, made of silk, with Greek inscription

Jane Almquist, the designer Frances Biggs. The vestments are made of wild silk. There is no ornamentation except the Greek inscriptions: 'remain in my love' (green), 'receive the Holy Spirit' (red), 'glory in the highest' (white), and 'come Lord Jesus' (violet). If one wishes to behold sheer elemental beauty, it is all here. The simplicity of the design and the richness of the material combine to make a garment worthy of the mystery that is being celebrated and of the leader of the assembly who takes the place of Christ. 'Art builds upon craft, giving to merely practical objects a quality of transcendence that links the material and the spiritual world. The work of the artists is not a superfluous luxury.' (Directory, p.13) The transcendence is all there in abundance. So is the music.

Michael Biggs

The overall design of the cathedral sanctuary is the brainchild of Michael Biggs and Gerald MacCann, the local architect selected by Bishop Duffy to direct the entire project. Biggs and MacCann understood and respected each other. They worked hand in hand for about ten years. Biggs had no sense of time. He was literally a genius when it came to design, shape and form. He had a marvellous nobility about him, a gentleness and charm that radiated from him, and was, as one would predict, a dreamer. MacCann felt perfectly at home in his company, burning the midnight oil together over detailed plans, changing and adapting, aiming at total perfection. Someone said about Biggs that he was like a man etched in stone but with a heart of flesh. He was in journeys often up and down to Monaghan. He ate and drank cathedral which became an ardent pursuit, the greatest work, he declared, that he had ever been asked to undertake. He came with a great pedigree behind him. As a young man he had learned his trade at the Guild

Bronze medallion on the cathedra

Craft Community workshop of Eric Gill at Ditchling in Surrey. Gill was one of the outstanding artists in his time as a sculptor, as a carver in stone and wood, as typeface designer, and graphic artist. Gill is reported to have said to a friend of his, David Jones: 'What I achieve as a sculptor is of no consequence – it can only be a beginning. It will take generations, but if only the beginnings of a reasonable, decent holy tradition of work might be effected.'

Michael marked such beginnings in Ireland. Was it more than first beginnings? Will any artist in this country ever excel Michael in his lettering on stone? The utter perfection of his lettering says a lot about the man. He was a perfectionist. He was a high priest of stone. He got to the heart of things. He used to say that the shape was already in the stone only to release it. He released many a stone across the country. He carved altars, ambos, sedelias, and fonts for many churches in Ireland. He took great pride in his huge granite altar in St Michael's, Dún Laoghaire, Co Dublin (1973), to be followed by St Conal's, Glenties, Co Donegal (1974), Holy Cross Abbey, Thurles, Co Tipperary (1975) and Star of the Sea Church, Rostrevor, Co Down (1990). One of his greatest feats must be the memorial inscriptional wall at Arbour Hill Cemetery, Dublin. He carved in English and in Irish the 5000 letters of the 1916 Proclamation (1960-63). His enormous contribution to the cathedral is described already in this book by Louis McRedmond. It takes the sight out of one's eyes to view the sanctuary area as one enters the cathedral.

Mystery

Michael wrestled with mystery all his life, with the mystery of the Trinity, with the union of the divine and the human in Christ, with the presence of Christ in the

Altar, ambo and crucifix

The Richard Enda King crucifix with
figure cast in bronze on oak

Eucharist. It reminds one of the verse from one of his favourite poets, Goethe: 'How great is that with which we wrestle and how little what we wrestle with.'

What cracked his doubts in the end and led him to be received into the Roman Catholic Church just a few days before he died? Whatever it was, it led to great peace. Michael passed away in perfect peace on 26 November 1993. All pain and anguish had disappeared from his body, the furrows from his brow, after a protracted and very painful illness. His aristocracy of soul was most evident. Evident too in his workmanship in the cathedral.

Richard Enda King

Richard Enda King (1942-1995) has left a distinctive imprint on the renewed sanctuary. King has several major sculptures to his credit, one among them being 'Spirit of the Air' for Dublin Airport roundabout, seventeen metres high in granite. His other three notable sculptures are in welded steel, 'Vigil' for Dún Laoghaire Fire Station, 'Evocation' for Athlone relief road, and 'The Fifth Province' for Navan relief road. King represented Ireland (1965-1977) in international exhibitions of metal and enamel sculpture in Cologne and Stuttgart, Germany; in stained glass at the New York World Fair; and at various liturgical art exhibitions in England and the USA.

The output of this gifted young artist over the span of twenty-three years was enormous. The materials employed included stone, metal, wood, glass, enamels and mixed media. He is represented in twenty-eight churches, religious houses and educational establishments, apart from hospitals, hotels and memorial sculptures.

His tabernacle in Monaghan Cathedral (see page 15) is an outstanding piece of reli-

gious art. Fr Laurence Flynn, priest of the diocese of Clogher and liturgist, states: 'The tabernacle is cast in bronze and plated in silver and gold. It suggests a tent, with the exodial and johannine motif of presence related to that image. Around it the words SOLAS DÉ flow as an uninterrupted river of life. Above and of a piece with it, a descending dove forms the holder for the lamp of the presence with its living flame. All of this rich symbolism is understated, if anything. Here is contemporary art well worthy of the mystery it serves, at once revealing and concealing, inviting contemplation and wonder.' It could hardly be stated better. The place and the setting into which it is inserted does invite contemplation and wonder. King had stated his own belief that the role of the religious artist is essentially in the service of renewal in the Church. The artist should attempt, through the method of material transformation, to express the deep spiritual and theological tenets of the faith in a manner which also assists in meeting the liturgical requirements and devotional aspirations of the people of God.

Innate quality of beauty and permanence was his criterion for his crucifix in the sanctuary area of the cathedral . The figure of Christ is cast in bronze by the lost wax method, a technique which reaches back to very ancient civilisations. He was conscious that in Ireland we are the inventors of a rich bronze working culture, as is evident in the treasures of the National Museum and elsewhere. The timber cross is entirely of solid oak, hewn from an (approx) two-hundred-year-old tree from Coolatin, Co Wicklow. It is composed of one single length, divided to form the upright and transom beam. Oak is a particularly fitting choice for its intrinsic strength and durability. The following is from Richard Enda's own personal meditations on the theological dimension of the crucified Christ, which he says is the very heart of the Christian belief and understanding of the

Godhead. He wrote: 'Our faith begins with the bleakness and foreboding which is the night of the cross. It is in the suffering of Christ, in his temptations and doubts in Gethsemane and in his abandonment by God on the cross, that we can identify with, and share with him in the eternal life of the resurrection. Christ in his forsakenness and death represents the infinite grief and love of the Father for the Son and for all humankind. Christ says, according to John 12:32: "And when I am lifted up from the earth I shall draw all men to myself".'

The Light of the World

King's own personal reflections on the passion of Christ show a profoundly contemplative mind and an exquisite humanity.

'Through his own abandonment the crucified Christ brings God to those who are forsaken. Through his suffering, he brings hopefulness to those who are in pain. Through his death, he brings eternal salvation to those who are dying. The sorrow of the love of the Father for the Son and for all humanity is, in a sense, the imperfectly understood power of the indwelling of the Holy Spirit, the infinitely redeeming source of the cross. Here in the flowing blood of the wounds of the hands and feet and the issuing of water from his side, are the signs of sanctifying grace, the sacramental efficacy of the Eucharist and of Baptism, signifying the Church of God, which is born like a second Eve from the side of a second Adam. Here in this figure of the dying Christ crowned with thorns I have attempted to show the ineluctable state in which he died on a cross of wood: that in his dying he had, and continues to have, the most infinite love for all his people, a love which, in the words of John 14:27, he offers us unconditionally:

The Eleventh Station. One of the entire set of Stations of the Cross in the cloister at the north end, painted in acrylic by Frances Biggs

"Peace I bequeath to you, my own peace I give you. A peace the world cannot give, this is my gift to you." I hope that this sense of peace is suitably conveyed, particularly in the face of Christ; that behind the transitory human pain and anguish resides the eternal serenity of his salvific existence.

The figure of the Christ was modelled in the wax of the paschal candle, and transformed in the purification of molten bronze, and perfected by the hands and mind of a believer in that Christ, who is the light of the world, and for the greater honour and glory of God.'

Richard Enda King died on 12 October 1995, an enormous loss for his wife Mary and for his family as well as for the Church and country. He had a rich and beautiful personality, a happiness of disposition and a golden tongue.

The Pietà

The Blessed Virgin Mary finds an honoured place in the cathedral, significantly near the entrance. The bronze Pietà is the work of Nell Murphy, another celebrated Irish artist. Nell was awarded a sculpture scholarship by the Irish Arts Council in 1954, enabling her to study at the Accademia delle Belle Arti in Florence. She studied sculpture for two semesters at the Hochschule für bildente Kunst, near Berlin, Germany, 1960-61, and enjoyed a further opportunity to study at the Richard Ginori School of Ceramics in Italy. Her work occupies a very wide span across Ireland using such varied mediums as hardwood, polychrome, Portland stone, bronze, cast concrete and cast alfresco. Her Stations of the Cross range from the North – Maghera and Toombridge, Co Derry, Belfast, Clogher, Co Tyrone, Glenties, Co Donegal, Murlog near Lifford – to the Midlands – Gormanston (Franciscan Cemetery), Laytown (Parish Church), Naas (Mercy Convent) – from the Midlands to Dublin (Kilmacud), and from Dublin down to the famous Fossa Church outside Killarney. Apart from the Stations of the Cross, her images of Mary with her uniquely sensitive style find a home in many Irish churches. One of her most distinctive works is the sculptured wall at Maghera in cast relief, showing the lives of the Irish saints.

Her cathedral *Pietà* (see page 81) represents a courageous middle-aged Mary holding her dead son and sharing the suffering of the human race. A very striking piece of sculpture, it combines both strength and tenderness which is typical of the woman portrayed in the gospel of John. The dark blue background comes alive with the bold silver white letters, of the text of the *Magnificat*, Mary's song of the poor. The lettering is the work of Michael Biggs.

A Local Craftsman

A local contribution to the cathedral tells its own story. Martin Leonard, of Leonard Engineering Company, Ballybay and Coolshannagh, Monaghan, executed the miniature bronze gates for the aumbry in the Chapel of the Holy Oils, which were designed by Michael Biggs. Apart from the excellence of the work, it invites one to gaze at length at so much beauty in such tiny dimensions. The craftsman belongs to generations of Leonards who contributed to the cathedral. Ask a silly question and you'll get the appropriate answer: 'Where did you train for this work?' 'I learned it from my father,' he rejoined. His grandfather had put the pegs in the walls for the Stations of the Cross in the cathedral. His great grandfather had worked on the chimes. Martin himself takes

Plaque in the vestibule of the Chapter House

great pride in the side entrance gates and railings, constructed by him in 1996. The Leonards belong to a long line of local artists including stone masons of the nineteenth century who were responsible for the foliated carving of the capitals and the carved heads on the corbel stones inside the building, and for much of the strikingly magnificent work on the outside.

'We like you as bishop. I hope you like us as artists.' The bishop liked all his artists. He takes great pride in their having set the seal on a work of re-ordering which is both daring and beautiful and will serve his people well as they journey in hope into the third millennium.

The Making of the Altar

CLIODNA CUSSEN

I KNEW Michael Biggs from the conversations we had together. Like most sculptors, he loved, when emerging from the cavern of his concentration, to meet a fellow sculptor and talk. The talk was wide-ranging, but mostly we talked about geometry, the nature of shape and line, the importance of mass, and the effect of sunlight falling on stone. We would stand among the quarry stones and rest ourselves talking of abstractions. Michael understood abstractions.

I never met him except in this context. I heard of him, of course, as one of the great, for at the beginning of the 60s there was a ferment among the stone sculptors of Dublin when word went out that Michael Biggs had got a big job doing the new altar stones for St Michael's, Dún Laoghaire, following the fire that necessitated re-building the church. Michael hired a lot of young sculptors to work on these huge abstract granite pieces. For many it was their first real contact with a big stone job; for many it was a kind of informal apprenticeship, a sort of early symposium. Modern stone sculpture in Ireland could be said to date from this time. In designing this altar, as in subsequent ones, Michael went for non-right-angled design. In an era devoted to square architectural boxes, he saw only curves of infinite subtlety.

Using fine-punched Dublin/Wicklow granite, he made curves flow into each other with only slight changes in planes and invisible gradations that showed up when the light fell slant-wise. He got a chance to use and extend his skill and perception in a series of works for new churches being built in the 60s, 70s and early 80s. On these jobs he put his feeling for mass and simplicity of line to good use. He belonged to a generation that had no feeling for the use of patterning or decoration; line and form were all.

He was a familiar figure in the granite quarries in Barr na Coille, Dublin. In Roe

and O'Neill's and Walsh's, a big Michael Biggs job was a cause for rejoicing all round. Rejoicing and trepidation too, for he was an exacting task master. For the men with the stone-cutting skills learned in the 80s – before Dublin Corporation stopped buying granite and the architects turned to concrete for everything, and the great decline in the stone trade started – Michael Biggs' jobs gave them a chance to show off their skills. Sometimes his search for perfection to within a quarter of an inch was too much for them.

On the Monaghan Cathedral job, one of the last real big ones, the making of Michael's 15-ton granite altar was given to Jim O'Neill, a superb stone mason. Jim brought the immense block to its final punched shape and Michael wanted to go further, into the very fine punching that makes granite look like plastic. Jim did not like this final ultimate softening, saying it would ruin the surface of the stone and was quite unnecessary, but Michael insisted, got out his tiny chisel and punched all over the surface himself, hunched over the huge block, tipping away day after day in the cold shed. Finished and set up in Monaghan Cathedral, the creamy white altar-stone seemed to float on air.

Michael looked for perfection. You could not imagine him walking away from a job saying 'It will do'. He finished everything with dedication, no half measures, no rushed jobs, only the most exacting criteria for everything.

He once told me he had seen a white rainbow when walking on a clear winter's night in the hills of South England with his friend William Trevor. In my knowledge of him there was this feeling of someone who had been looking for a white rainbow or other magical occurrence all his life and had sometimes seen it.

In the huge amount of lettering he did, as in his sculpture, form was all-important, as was the depth of the line and the angle of the cut. Clarity, simplicity and gracefulness are the hallmarks of a Michael Biggs job.

He held classes in Kiltiernan in the early 80s, and anyone who went will still talk of what Michael Biggs would do or say when starting a present job. For him, geometry and rhythm in letters were as one. His alphabets are still in use. Wherever a panel of beautiful hand-cut letters are found from the 60s and 70s, it is almost certain to be a Michael Biggs job. Those who learned from him, Tom Little, Tom Glendon, are all fierce perfectionists in their own way.

One of our most interesting conversations was about the geometrical basis of Celtic design. I was doing a replacement Celtic cross for Cashel and I wondered if the basis of Celtic design was the circle. No, said Michael, it is the oval, the basis of Celtic design is elliptical. This was so true that it has since remained in my mind. Michael's voice, like that of any good teacher, had a way of staying in your ear.

He used the rhythm of the curve in his work, but he did not work on interior curves caused by piercing the stone form. He was very much of his time in using light as it plays on the planes of the surface and not as it plays on opened interior space.

Other times have other observations. There is no room for improvement in his work. It is just as it is – there, excellent, completely finished.

A Monstrance for St Macartan's Cathedral

RICHARD ENDA KING

THE MONSTRANCE, a circular, hand-raised and planished silver bowl of 175mm diameter (7 inches), and 60mm (2.5″) in height, contains within its centre a removable, silver, gilt-hinged circular pyx with a glass front, 80mm in diameter (3.5″) and 25mm in height (1″). Within the hinged pyx the facility is provided for two forms of lunette holders. One a manual ring form to secure the unbroken host, and when this is removed, the second one permanently hinged and secured to provide for the various compositional arrangements which the fragmented host will express. To further visually emphasise the broken host, a circular, deep blue vitreous enamelled silver disc, (kiln fused at 850 centigrade) is incorporated and appears only in the areas of hiatuses, contrasting with the whiteness of the broken host.

In conclusion, may I describe in imaginative terms my response to what I would hope will be complementary to your creative vision in this unique Monstrance concept? Gathered around the basket of divine fruit, the faithful would meditate on and sense the subtle nuance of God's natural reflected white light shimmering in the planished facets of silver. The interior gilt giving an aura of radiating warmth, surrounds the symbolic yellow stole of Christ's priesthood, which is enveloped in the gold pyx. Within the emission of spiritual presence, the universal centre of eucharistic sacramentality contained in the white host, is pierced only by a glimpse of the symbolic blue of the infinity and divinity of Christ.

Richard Enda King to Bishop Joseph Duffy, July 1995, three months before his death on 12 October 1995.

The Original Statuary

JOSEPH DUFFY

THE STATUES of the cathedral, both outside and inside, are the work of Carrara sculptors employed directly by Bishop Donnelly. Like the stained glass, they were considered not as individual works of merit but as a set of furnishings required to complete the cathedral.

The main central door is flanked by statues of SS Peter and Paul, set into niches. In the tympanum above the door is a relief of Christ giving the keys to Peter the shepherd, with a flock of sheep and palm trees.

On the west side of the tower is a Crowned Virgin, matched on the south by a Christ with his hand raised in blessing. In the tympanum over the south door is a relief of Virgin and Child surrounded by angels' heads and wings.

Still on the south side, the transept gable has a seven-niche arcade with life-size statues (see page 22). These are, from left to right:

1. St Tiarnach of Clones, honoured as successor of Macartan and Bishop of Clogher.
2. St Ultan of Ardbraccan, honoured as patron of children and Bishop of Clogher.
3. St Colmcille of Derry and Iona, patron of Ireland and founder of monasteries.
4. St Dympna of Gheel in Belgium and associated with Tydavnet.
5. Heber MacMahon, warrior-Bishop of Clogher in the seventeenth century.
6. Charles MacNally, Bishop of Clogher (1844-64) and founder of the cathedral, with a rudimentary model of the cathedral in his hand.
7. James Donnelly, Bishop of Clogher (1864-93), holding a complete model of the cathedral.

The north transept has a corresponding arcade (see page 41), with figures from the Old Testament in characteristic poses and displaying plenty of movement:

1. Abraham with his staff.
2. Moses with scroll and tablet.
3. David with lyre.
4. Isaiah with tablet reading *ecce virgo concipiet* (behold a virgin will conceive).
5. Jeremiah appealing for help with arms outstretched.
6. St Joachim with book (in the likeness of Pope Leo XIII).
7. St Anne with Mary as a child at her side learning to read.

Inside the north door of the Chapter House is a statue of St Benedict Joseph Labre (see page 74), the beggar saint of the eighteenth century to whom Bishop Donnelly had a personal devotion.

At the entrance to the north transept is a robust figure of St John the Baptist with a lamb at his feet.

On either side of the door from the tower porch into the south side aisle are SS Patrick and Brigid, first and second patrons of Ireland. Patrick is shown spurning snakes and holding a shamrock, Brigid with a book and the short staff of an abbess.

The statue of St Benedict Joseph Labre cast in Carrara marble adorning the entrance to the Chapter House

The Stained Glass

JOSEPH DUFFY

THE STAINED glass in the cathedral was made by three different firms between 1884 and 1892, the year of dedication: Meyer of Munich, Earley and Powell of Dublin, and Cox and Buckley of Youghal. The themes for all the windows were decided by Bishop Donnelly himself, who also found the donors whose names appear on the windows. It is clear from his correspondence that the bishop was less than happy with any of the three firms for the quality of their workmanship. The themes, on the other hand, give us a good compendium of the devotional life of the late nineteenth century, including the bishop's partiality for John the Baptist and Benedict Joseph Labre.

Apse

Seven windows by Meyer, reading from left to right:

1. Annunciation, Nativity, Adoration of the Magi, Presentation in the Temple.
2. Finding in the Temple, Baptism of our Lord, Marriage feast at Cana, Sermon on the Mount.
3. Promise of the Keys, Transfiguration, Last Supper, Agony in the Garden.
4. Crucifixion (with mullion removed for greater clarity).
5. Resurrection, Ascension, Descent of the Holy Spirit, St Peter preaching in Jerusalem.
6. Martyrdom of St Stephen, Conversion of St Paul, Martyrdom of St Peter with view of pagan Rome, Pope ruling in Rome, present St Peter's, modern Rome, Pope on Easter Sunday blessing all.
7. Mission of St Patrick by Pope Celestine, St Patrick preaching at Tara, with king, princes, druids, fire, shamrock, snakes etc., Consecration of St Macartan (in the

likeness of Bishop MacNally), Dedication of this cathedral with the people, town, cathedral itself, Bishop of Clogher, Archbishops of Armagh, Cashel and Dublin.

Chapel of Blessed Sacrament
Window by Earley and Powell.

Sacred Heart of Jesus in centre surrounded by eucharistic symbols. On left Melchizedek king of Salem blessing bread and wine over Abraham and his soldiers returning from battle. On the right Abraham about to slay his son Isaac in sacrifice before being restrained by the angel. In the circlets above are a lamb denoting the Paschal Lamb of the Old Testament, a pelican, the bird that gives its blood to feed its young, and at the top a priest holding up the sacred host at the elevation of the Mass with his back to the people.

The coat of arms and motto are of Andrew Clark of Leith in Scotland and relative of an earlier Bishop of Clogher, James Murphy. This was the first window in the cathedral to be 'glassed.'

Chapel of Reconciliation
Three windows, first by Earley and Powell, second and third by Cox and Buckley.
1.   St Benedict Joseph Labre in the centre with the symbols of his special charism: his staff for he spent much time walking the roads; his wallet which contained his New Testament and breviary and a few papers by which he was identified after his death; a large rosary which he carried round his neck; and his hands joined in prayer.

On the left is described the incident of his being sent away from the Trappist monastery in the north of France where he had walked 60 miles from his home, only to be refused permission to become a Trappist. The minimum age was 24 and he was only 20. His vocation was elsewhere.

On the right we see Benedict on the last day of his life, 16 April 1783, Wednesday of Holy Week. He has fainted on the steps of the Church of Santa Maria dei Monti in Rome. A local butcher named Zaccarelli recognised him and came to his help as did others who were passing by. Benedict agreed to be taken to Zaccarelli's house where he died later that day.

The medallion window at the top shows Benedict praying in the presence of the Blessed Sacrament exposed in the Monstrance. Two angels over the centrepiece carry a scroll inscribed 'Blessed are the poor in spirit for theirs is the kingdom of heaven'.

Three small windows underneath show typical scenes in the saint's life: walking on the roads of Italy with a church as his destination, the Basilica of Loreto where he spent Holy Week for 11 successive years at the Holy House, the Colosseum in Rome which he loved because of the Christian martyrs buried there.

2. Two scenes from the life of St Dympna. Scene one is her profession of faith. Rejecting the proposals of her frenzied father who had, according to legend, followed her from Ireland to Gheel in Belgium, she professes her faith publicly. In scene two her father in anger slays his 15-year old daughter.

   Dympna is the patroness of the mentally afflicted and since the seventeenth century has been popularly identified with Davnet of Tydavnet. The artist has tried to copy details of old Irish dress. The shamrock is used in the base with branches of lilies and palms. The circle in the top shows an angel with a heavenly crown while lilies spring up in the cinquefoil, emblems of Dympna, virgin and martyr.

*The Rose window on the organ gallery
as seen from the sanctuary*

3. SS John the Evangelist and James the Greater. John is shown writing the Apocalypse with pen in hand and the mystical eagle near him. James is dressed as a pilgrim as he is usually represented, e.g. his association with Compostela in Spain. His other emblem, the escallop shell, is seen in the cinquefoil of the circle at the top. James is mentioned as the first of the disciples to go on a missionary journey. The escallop shells refer to pilgrimage.

    In the circle is John standing by the cross with Mary the Mother of God and Mary Magdalen kneeling at the foot of the cross.

South Aisle

Four windows, all by Meyer except the second which is by Cox and Buckley.

1. St Anne and Our Lady.
2. SS Bartholomew and Thomas, apostles. Bartholomew is shown with a flaying knife and Thomas with a carpenter's square, as the patron of builders. Each is carrying a book. In the centre are shown the Unbelief of Thomas (above) and the Martyrdom of Bartholomew (below). In the circle at the top is an angel praying.
3. SS Dabheocus, Ultan and Lassera, a group of Clogher saints. Davog was the founder and first abbot of Lough Derg. Ultan was an early Bishop of Clogher according to the Clogher Register. Lassera was an abbess and known as Lastra in the parish of Donaghmoyne where her cult survives at a holy well. The sexfoil at the top shows Station Island, Lough Derg, the most important shrine in the diocese of Clogher.
4. SS Elizabeth, Michael and Catherine. Elizabeth of Hungary was a youthful queen of the thirteenth century who devoted her life to the sick and the poor before dying

at the age of 24. The cult of Michael the archangel began in the East where he was invoked for the care of the sick. Catherine of Alexandria, identifiable by the wheel, was invoked as protectress of the dying.

West Wall
Three windows, two over side doors by Meyer, rose window by Cox and Buckley.
1. Over south door. SS Benedict, Francis of Assisi, Alphonsus Liguori and Dominic, founders of religious orders. Benedict is famous for his rule, Francis for his poverty, Alphonsus for his preaching and teaching (he founded the Redemptorists), and Dominic for the rosary.
2. Rose window over Organ gallery. In the centre is the Sacred Heart, shedding rays of glory all round the circumference. In the circlets are the emblems of Our Lady from the Litany of Loreto, e.g. Morning Star, Tower of Ivory, Seat of Justice etc. The outer circle is a series of converging arcades in jewelled glass.
3. Over north door, SS Stanislaus Kostka, Francis Xavier, Ignatius Loyola and Aloysius Gonzaga, are sixteenth-century Jesuit saints. Stanislaus was a Polish novice who died at the age of 18. Francis was a missionary in the Far East. Ignatius was the founder of the order. Aloysius became patron of youth.

Lady Chapel (formerly the baptistery)
Five windows depicting scenes from the life of John the Baptist, all by Meyer.
1. Apparition of the Angel Gabriel to Zechariah in the Temple announcing that he would have a son to be called John.

Pietà by Nell Murphy, with lettering by Michael Biggs

Holy Family of Nazareth by Meyer of Munich

2. Visit of the Blessed Virgin Mary to the house of Zechariah with Elizabeth and Zechariah meeting Mary at the entrance of their home.
3. John the Baptist baptising Jesus in the Jordan.
4. John preaching to the people in the desert by the Jordan.
5. Salome bringing the head of John on a dish to Herod.

North Aisle

Four windows, three by Meyer, the fourth by Cox and Buckley.

1. SS Jerome, Gregory the Great, Augustine, and John Chrysostom, doctors of the Church. Jerome in sexfoil, dressed as a cardinal, and writing with the aid of a dove, symbol of the Holy Spirit. Gregory, dressed in cope and tiara of the Pope, with the three-crossbar staff, sign of his office as Pope. Augustine, described as the most influential Christian writer after St Paul. John Chrysostom, the fourth-century Archbishop of Constantinople and one of the Greek doctors of the Church.
2. SS Molaisse, Tighearnach and Fanchea, a group of Clogher saints. Molaisse was the founder and first abbot of the great monastery of Devenish. Tighearnach (or Tiarnach) founded the monastery of Clones. Fanchea was an abbess associated with Rossorry near Enniskillen. The sexfoil shows the ruined round tower of Devenish, which may be seen today on Lower Lough Erne.
3. SS Patrick, Brigid and Columcille, the three patrons of Ireland. The sexfoil shows Patrick landing in Ireland as bishop.
4. SS Peter and James the Lesser, apostles. Peter has his key and James his club of martyrdom. In the centre are two scenes from their lives: the upper showing Jesus

giving charge of his flock to Peter, 'Feed my lambs'; and the lower the martyrdom of James. The sexfoil has an angel praying.

North Transept

Window, depicting the Holy Family of Nazareth, by Meyer.

Chapel of Holy Oils

Window by Earley and Powell.

St Joseph in centre holding a flower with inscription underneath: *Ite ad Joseph* (Go to Joseph). On the left the betrothal of Mary and Joseph in the presence of God the Father. On the right the flight into Egypt. In the circle at the top two angels with a scroll which reads: *Te Joseph celebrant agmina coelorum* (The hosts of heaven celebrate you, O Joseph.)

The Baptistery

Window by Earley and Powell.

Mary and Child in centre with inscription underneath: Mother of God pray for us. On the left the adoration of the Magi. On the right the adoration of the shepherds. In the circle at the top two angels with a scroll which reads *Gloria in excelsis Deo* (Glory to God on high).

A Patron for Passers-by: Benedict Joseph Labre

JOSEPH DUFFY

THE STAINED GLASS windows and statues of the cathedral are a catalogue of our Christian past, a litany to more than forty holy men and women who join our liturgy from another world. One of them, Benedict Joseph Labre, might be considered the patron of visitors who drop in to say a private prayer, or to make a quiet visit to the Blessed Sacrament. He gets special attention in Monaghan Cathedral for a reason that belongs to its history. He died in Rome on 16 April 1783.

In 1864, three years after the foundation stone of the cathedral had been laid, James Donnelly became Bishop of Clogher. The walls were barely above the ground at the time and all the indications were that progress would continue to be extremely slow. The work was done by direct labour and by the time-honoured means of shovel and spade and horse and cart. Moreover, the building fund was perpetually low. And when the money ran out, as it often did, the work ground to a halt altogether.

Small wonder then that the bishop went to Rome in 1867 for his first visit there, with no end in sight for his enterprise. He records in his diary how he offered Mass at the tomb of Benedict Joseph Labre and prayed for the completion of the cathedral through his intercession. Furthermore, he promised to honour his memory in the cathedral if he would live to see the building completed and the holy man canonised. By 1892 both events had come to pass and the bishop kept his word. A fine statue in Carrara marble adorns the hallway of the Chapter House (see page 74), and the story of the saint's life is told in the window of the Reconciliation Chapel.

Who was this Benedict Joseph Labre? I discovered him for myself during my first summer holidays as bishop, in 1980. In the company of a friend of long standing, a Frenchman with a noble Fermanagh surname, Gilbert Tierny, we drove into the small village of Amettes in the north-east corner of France. Gilbert remarked casually that we were in the birthplace of Benedict Joseph Labre. I was not at all prepared for this as I had always associated Benedict with the Colosseum in Rome where he spent the last years of his life, in the place associated with the early Christian martyrs. We stopped the car and went to see the little house where Benedict was born. The eighteenth-century layout and bits of furniture were carefully preserved – a simple hearth, small wooden chairs, a few narrow beds. Given the size of the house, we were surprised to learn that Benedict's parents belonged to the middle class and were able to send their fifteen children, of whom Benedict was the eldest, to the local school run by the priest of the parish.

Benedict left this house at the age of twelve to stay with a priest-uncle who took over his education. On the death of his uncle six years later, Benedict returned home and left finally at the age of 21 in search of a monastery where he would become a monk. He was everywhere turned down until it gradually became clear to him that his calling was elsewhere. He was to remain a layman in the world; but he would lead a totally new kind of religious life, that of a pilgrim-hermit. This meant taking to the road on his own, pilgrim staff in hand and literally nothing else apart from the clothes he wore, a few religious books and rosary beads. He set out to visit in turn the famous Christian shrines of the day and broke his journey only to call into churches on the way. Over seven years he visited, on foot, most of the great shrines of Europe: Loreto, Assisi, Naples, Bari, Fabriano in Italy; Einsiedeln in Switzerland; Compostela in Spain; Paray-le-Monial in France. The rest of his life he spent in Rome, leaving only once a year to visit the Holy House of Loreto. He lived a life of deliberate and extreme poverty, never begging but living on left-overs or on what he was given, and sharing even that. He died of total physical exhaustion at the age of 35 . On the evening of his death, the children cried out in the streets of Rome: 'The saint is dead.'

ORATE PRO ANIMABUS
EPISCOPORUM
DIOCESIS
CLOGHERENSIS
QUORUM CORPORA HIC
IN PACE REQUIESCUNT.

ILLMI ET REVMI D. CAROLI McNALLY
QUI HANC ECCLESIAM CATHEDRALEM
FUNDAVIT ET MUNERE EPISCOPATUS PER
XXI ANNOS FUNCTUS DIE XXVII NOVEMBRIS
MDCCCLXIV ANNOS LXXXI NATUS OBDORMIVIT
IN DOMINO;

ILLMI ET REVMI D. JACOBI DONNELLY
QUI POSTQUAM ECCLESIAM CATHEDRALEM JAM
INCHOATAM, STUDIO SUO INDEFESSO PERFECTAM
ATQUE ORNATAM REDITIBUSQUE DOTATAM, DEO
FAVENTE DEDICAVIT, ANNUM SEPTUAGESIMUM
TERTIUM SUÆ ÆTATIS, EPISCOPATUS VERO
ANNUM VICESIMUM NONUM AGENS DIE XXIX
DECEMBRIS MDCCCXCIII DIEM SUPREMUM
PIE OBIIT;

ILLMI ET REVMI D. RICARDI OWENS
QUI ÆDES EPISCOPALES EXSTRUENDO OPERA
ANTECESSORUM FELICITER COMPLEVIT AC PER
ANNOS FERE XV EPISCOPATUS OFFICIIS ASSIDUE
DEDITUS, ANNOS LXIX NATUS E VITA EXCESSIT
DIE III MARTII MDCCCCIX.

ILLMI ET REVMI D. PATRITII McKENNA
QUI IN MUNERE EPISCOPALI PER XXXIII
FERE ANNOS CLARE LABORIOSEQUE VERSATUS,
GREGEM DILIGENTER PASCEBAT BENIGNEQUE
FOVEBAT. ET, MULTIS PER TOTAM
DIOCESIM AEDIFICIIS AD DEI GLORIAM
EXIMIO ZELO SUO ERECTIS RENOVATISQUE,
ANNOS LXXIII NATUS, DIE VII FEBRUARII
MCMXLII ANIMAM DEO REDDIDIT.

Benedict was in the tradition of the early hermits of the desert and of those heroic Celtic monks who, like him, also left father and mother, home and country to wander over the European mainland. His radical brand of spirituality was, and remains, utterly counter-cultural. When the Holy See bowed to public demand and opened his cause for beatification within a month of his death, the rich and the powerful were profoundly shocked. The French ambassador to Rome, Cardinal de Bernis, wrote derisively of the pious comedy which he presumed, rightly, would not be quickly forgotten. There were rumblings that the Jesuits, then recently expelled from Rome, were at the back of it. The philosophical world of the Enlightenment, that glittering world of the pre-French Revolution intelligentsia, which exalted reason, order, and elegance to the exclusion of all else, was horrified that attention should be given to an obscure vagabond who had made no contribution to society and who was, in addition, an unhygienic nuisance.

Benedict's way of life was indeed highly unconventional, even in those rough times, and he was never likely to be widely understood, much less attract a following. All he wanted in life was time and space to be with God. Any other consideration was incidental. We can only imagine how much it cost him, but ultimately it did not matter to him that he had no job or lost contact with his family, or that he was often without food or shelter, even in his final bouts of illness. For a man who spent so much time in church, his links with the clergy were minimal. In fact, they seem to have been confined to taking regular advice from experienced confessors and this only to reassure himself that his calling was genuinely from God. He would then return to the silence and solitude of the place where he was most truly himself, the ever-living presence of his Lord in the Blessed Sacrament.

Cathedral and Mission

BRENDAN COONEY

WHEN POPE John Paul II visited Ireland in 1979, he spoke to many seminarians, clergy and laity in the great chapel of Maynooth. He reminded all present that a local Church is essentially missionary in nature: 'May the spirit of partnership grow between the home dioceses and the home religious congregations in the total mission of the Church, until each local diocesan Church and each religious congregation and community is fully seen to be missionary of its very nature.' Many priests, brothers, sisters and lay men and women, natives of Clogher diocese, have joined missionary societies and congregations and gone out to work in countries all over the world. A number of priests became 'volunteer' missionaries for a number of years with missionary societies such as the Columbans and the Kiltegan Fathers and did heroic work, often in very difficult conditions.

In 1984 the diocese of Clogher officially entered into partnership with the diocese of Kitui in Kenya through St Patrick's Missionary Society, Kiltegan. The partnership involved some Clogher diocesan priests serving in Kenya for a number of years and then being replaced by other Clogher priests. The Mercy sisters from the diocese also responded and, in these closing years of the second millennium, both Clogher priests and sisters are still offering sterling service in the diocese of Kitui, Kenya. Until 1996, that diocese was administered by Westmeath-born Bishop William Dunne. The Clogher-Kitui partnership continues with the new Bishop of Kitui, Boniface Lele. In January 1985 Monaghan Cathedral hosted the first official mission commissioning ceremony, when the first Clogher priests to work in Kenya under the new partnership scheme, Patrick McDonnell and Vincent Connolly, were officially mandated to go forth and preach the gospel, in season and out of season, in Kitui, Kenya. In 1990 the

Stations of the Cross in the cloister at the north end

cathedral again witnessed the commissioning of two replacement priests, Laurence Duffy and Terence McElvaney who continued the work of the first two priests. Archbishop Pantin of Trinidad preached at this commissioning. In 1994 there was a further commissioning in the cathedral of Fathers Laurence Flynn and Hubert Martin, at which Fr Ribero of Zanzibar preached. 1986 and 1996 saw the commissioning of Sisters Marie Evans and Marie Cox, both of Our Lady of Mercy, Castleblayney. Lay missionaries from Monaghan have also worked in Africa and South America. Mary Duffy and Mary Clerkin are fine examples of Legion of Mary envoys.

Each year Monaghan Cathedral hosts a missionary society or congregation at one weekend of Masses. Members of these organisations keep the people of the diocese informed of the work that nearly 4,000 Irish missionaries are doing in 97 countries around the world. The other churches in the diocese also get a chance to hear about this work. The diocese also supports this work in many practical ways – prayer, financial resources and the many-faceted assistance of the Apostolic Work Society. This, of course, is in keeping with the missionary decree of the Second Vatican Council which states: 'It will be very useful for a community to maintain contact with missionaries who come from its ranks, or with some parish or diocese in the missions' (*Ad Gentes*). When we remember that the cathedral is the seat of the bishop then another statement of this document, *Ad Gentes*, is particularly apt: 'All bishops are consecrated not just for one diocese but for the salvation of the whole world.' Monaghan Cathedral, therefore, can be said to serve a three-fold purpose. First, it is the seat of the Church of the diocese of Clogher and thus serves all the people of the diocese, north and south of the border; second, it is a parish church for the parish of Monaghan town; third, it is the epicentre for the Church of Clogher in efforts 'for the salvation of the entire world'.

The power of the cathedral in sharing the message of Jesus Christ outside the diocese of Clogher was shown not only in the mission commissioning ceremonies of 1985 to 1996, but also in 1990 during the Holy Week ceremonies, televised by Eurovision and watched by many millions throughout Europe. The recent refurbishment of the sanctuary was ideal for the ceremonies and showed off both the breadth of the sanctuary and the splendour of the Easter ceremonies in the best possible light. The broad sweep of the sanctuary should be understood in its cathedral function rather than in its parish function. Here in the sanctuary all the priests of the diocese can gather with the bishop and the people can, even as in the days of Zechariah in the sanctuary of the Temple, experience the sacredness of the sanctuary of the Lord. It is not so much the empty cathedral which gives a sense of the all-embracing message and sacrament of Jesus Christ, but the cathedral filled with people giving praise to God and praying that all people, all over the world, may know the mighty power and the restful peace of Jesus the Lord.

The Renewal: A Personal Reflection

An tEaspag cct.

I heard the call
of this heavenly hall,
and in I came.
And there I was, in endless doubt,
uselessly turning over my darkness,
until sharply summoned by the strong light
from the morning sun
to show my hand.
I then adopted this stone offering
rising under the canopy of heaven,
a challenge to confusion, to misgivings,
to the to-ings and fro-ings of my waverings.

Lord, to petty idols
I have too often
presented eyes promised to your brightness.
I have too often worn away uncertain steps
on night ways. But, Lord, today
I am restored to a joy of life.
Your light sweeps over me like a cleansing wave
to reveal
recesses I had never seen,
timid secrets of desire,
the boundless freedom of generous hearts,
also searching for you,
light of light.

The Contributors

Brendan Cooney is Director of the Irish Missionary Union. Has ministered in Kenya and in South Africa.

Cliodna Cussen, artist and sculptor, lives in Dublin.

✠ **Joseph Duffy** was ordained Bishop of Clogher on 2 September 1979. An historian and Celtic scholar, he is former Chairman of the National Liturgical Commission

Mildred Dunne is a doctoral student in the History of Art Department, Trinity College, Dublin.

Austin Flannery O. P., Dominican Publications, Dublin, is editor of *Religious Life Review* and of *Vatican II: Conciliar and post Conciliar documents*.

Eltin Griffin O. Carm. (Editor and contributor) is a liturgist, a writer and a preacher.

Ambrose Macaulay, historian, is Parish Priest of St Brigid's, Derryvolgie Avenue, Belfast.

Gerald MacCann, architect to the Cathedral, belongs to a family firm of architects in Monaghan.

Louis McRedmond is a journalist, historian and lawyer.